IMAGES OF

Painswick,
Sheepscombe,
Slad & Edge

THE STREAM, SHEEPSCOMBE, c. 1918. Mrs Workman is seated in front of the cottages which now form the village hall. Winston Workman – ready with his jam jar – and Joyce Hogg try their hand at catching minnows.

Previous page: ALL DRESSED UP. In this Edwardian scene, taken at a Clipping Service (see page 14), Painswick townspeople are seen in their Sunday best clothes. Notice the ladies' hats and the flowers in the children's hair.

IMAGES OF ENGLAND

Painswick, Sheepscombe, Slad & Edge

Howard Beard

NONSUCH

PADDLING, c. 1932. Taken at the same spot as the picture on page 2, this delightful photograph shows a new generation of village youngsters. They are, left to right, Fay West (partly hidden), Arthur Herbert, Neville West, Frances Light, Marion Light, Alan Smith, Janet Smith and Eva Herbert. The cottage on the left had been rebuilt since the earlier view was taken.

Front cover illustration: The Falcon Bowling Club, Painswick, c. 1900.

First published 1997
This new pocket edition 2006
Images unchanged from first edition

Nonsuch Publishing Limited
The Mill, Brimscombe Port,
Stroud, Gloucestershire, GL5 2QG
www.nonsuch-publishing.com

Nonsuch Publishing is an imprint of Tempus Publishing Group

British Library Cataloguing in Publication Data.
A catalogue record for this book is available from the British Library.

ISBN 1-84588-304-7

Typesetting and origination by Nonsuch Publishing Limited
Printed in Great Britain by Oaklands Book Services Limited

WASHBROOK LANE, 1899. In this pleasingly composed early picture by Oscar Owers (see page 30) the photographer's wife is shown in the foreground.

Contents

THOMAS AND MARY HANKS.
Thomas was born around 1848 and lived in Butt Green, Painswick. This delightful photograph was taken *c.* 1900.

Acknowledgements

The author wishes to thank all those who helped in any way with the compilation of this book:

R. Alder, D. Archard, Mrs P. Berry, T. Berry, Mrs P. Blandford, Mrs H. Briggs, D. Burton, Mrs L. Coleman, D. Cope, the late Mrs M. Curtis, E. Cuss, Mrs A. Daniels, G. Emrys-Roberts, J. Fern, Mrs T. Greening, P. Griffin, P. Griffiths, the late Cdr B. Jones, Mrs J. Jones, Miss C. Kemp, Mrs C. Lavy, G. Luker, Mrs N. Marriott, W. Merrett, S. Mills, the late G. Moore, C. Muller, Mrs H. Musty, National Motor Museum at Beaulieu, Mr and Mrs J. Newiss, the late Mrs M. Payne, H. Pearce, Peckhams of Stroud Ltd, Mrs P. Perrins, T. Radway, Mrs P. Reynolds, the late B. Ricketts, the late H. Robinson, R. Shaw, J. Smith, Mrs B. Spring, Stroud News and Journal Ltd, A. Swain, D. Thomas, H. Twinning, Mrs I.Venn, Mrs J. Webb, Mrs B. Whitting and the Trustees of Brookthorpe Village Hall. Especial thanks also to Mrs E. Skinner and Mrs E.Harris of the Sheepscombe Historical Society.

Finally, my grateful thanks to my wife, Sylvia, for her constant help, advice and encouragement.

PAINSWICK, TWO EARLY VIEWS. The picture on the left is taken from F. Gyde's drawing of the Old Town Hall, built in the mid-17th century and demolished c. 1840. The view on the right dates from around 1875 to 1880 and is by Stroud photographer Oliver Smith. Note the relatively small size of the yew trees. The external gallery steps are just visible on the original photograph; they were removed in 1883.

Introduction

The ancient market town of Painswick has been called 'The Queen of the Cotswolds', a title which many would say it justly deserves, and its charms are enhanced by the attractive countryside in which it is set, as many of the photographs in the following pages demonstrate. Reputedly deriving its name from Pain Fitzjohn, Lord of the Manor of Wyke during the reign of King Stephen, the parish of Painswick extended in former times over a considerable area. However, as with neighbouring Bisley and Minchinhampton, it was subdivided during the nineteenth century, creating the new parishes of Sheepscombe, Slad, Edge and Uplands. The first three of these, together with Painswick itself, constitute the geographical limits of this book.

The date range of pictures selected for inclusion in the following pages is from the last quarter of the nineteenth century through to around 1950. By the early 1870s, photographers Paul and Oliver Smith had included churches around Painswick in their survey of the ecclesiastical buildings of the district (see pages 49 and 65). From the 1880s come early views of St Mary's Church. By the 1890s the private ownership of cameras was more common and several images from this period have been included, notably the Maitland Collection from Edge. With the advent in 1902 of the craze for picture postcards, the range of material to choose from became suddenly more plentiful and, as the last century progressed, the availability of good photographs increased dramatically.

The detail visible on photographs does not depend on their age: with the excellent lenses available to our Victorian forebears, clear, well-focused images were obtained that were often unmatched by those taken with the cheaper, mass-produced cameras of succeeding generations. As collectors will readily testify, there is a certain excitement in handling a really fine early print of high quality and definition.

Subject matter has also been an important consideration in choosing what to include. This book has attempted to use the best available examples of pictures illustrating social history rather than architecture. It is not within the scope of this volume to study and record the many fine and important buildings which the Painswick area contains; the author's intention has been rather to depict rural life as it was – costume, transport, events and pastimes. The earliest coherent group of pictures is of Edge villagers in the last years of the nineteenth century: the significance of these photographs is that they show ordinary people in their workaday clothes – cobblers, gardeners, housewives and children. Many wear bonnets or trousers which were already old-fashioned by the 1890s and had vanished by the period, a generation later, described in Cider with Rosie.

In the course of researching the background to the pictures – and especially in attempting to name children on school photographs – the author has met many fascinating people, experts in the history of their own town, village or hamlet. They have passed on information and anecdotes which bring the pictures vividly to life – for example, the parrot kept by the Misses Wemyss (see page 29).

Examining local newspaper archives for background information has been equally rewarding: the story of the George V Coronation Arch at The Vatch (page 77), for instance, needs to be set in the context of that great day of national celebration in the summer of 1911. The full significance of so many events often becomes clear only by reference to local press reports.

Compiling such a book as this is a thoroughly pleasurable experience. In addition to deepening one's knowledge of an attractive and unspoilt corner of Gloucestershire, there is the satisfaction of selecting, comparing and grouping photographs – also of rearranging them when better pictures come to light. Perhaps most rewarding of all is ensuring, through their publication, that images which document important areas of social history are not lost to posterity.

NEW STREET, PAINSWICK, c. 1905. The pedestrian is thought to be Rowland Smith, who ran a butcher's business in the town. The small shop immediately behind him is Albert Luker's hairdressing salon.

One

Painswick

PAINSWICK, c. 1910. Here the town is seen from a natural vantage point along the old road leading to Stroud. Newtown is in the foreground, with the Swiss Cottage easily distinguishable. Hale Ground has not yet been developed. Note, far right, Woodborough, recently built by a Mr Windle. Because of problems with springs in the hillside, substantial foundations were needed for this property.

NEW STREET, *c.* 1910. The tradesman standing on the pavement taking a breath of fresh air may possibly be the fishmonger whose shop-front is remembered as being adorned with a large painted salmon. The second building along on the left was Warner's Stores.

NEW STREET IN FESTIVE MOOD. The two girls on the right are sisters Mabel (left) and Melville Ireland. Melville was born in 1900, which would date the photograph to around 1903 or 1904, though it is just possible that it could show the town decorated for the Coronation of Edward VII in June 1902. The postcard from which this picture is taken is a truly delightful one, although it has not survived in pristine condition.

THE POST OFFICE, *c.* 1907. This building, later Walklett's Bakery, served as Painswick's post office until 1933. At the time this picture was produced Edward Spring was Postmaster, combining his duties with those of grocer, as the advertisements prove. Notice the display of postcards visible on the wall outside the shop.

NEW STREET, *c.* 1935. The post office has now moved into the half-timbered building it still occupies today. Built in 1478, it is claimed to be the oldest premises in the country actually housing a post office. Note the gas lamp, the petrol pumps for Horne's garage and, in the distance, the service bus ready to depart for Stroud. Mr Strange, the Postmaster when this photograph was taken, married the daughter of Edward Spring. In August 1997 Painswick post office featured on the 26p stamp celebrating the centenary of the National Federation of Sub-Postmasters.

THE MUDRAKERS. Cleaning Painswick's streets was mainly the responsibility of the Parish Council. However, New Street was the concern of the County Council. In 1901 the latter apparently failed in its duty and a group of townspeople calling themselves the Mudrakers met outside the Town Hall and set off to put the County Council to shame. Here they are seen posing in New Street for the photographer.

JACK MUSGROVE'S SHOP, c. 1934. The Musgrove family kept this shop for many years and it was a familiar sight in the town. Jack began his business in a small way around 1924, mending punctures. By the 1930s he also sold petrol. Standing in front of the pump are, left to right, Jack Musgrove, his elder daughter Joyce and Donald Cooke, his brother-in-law. The shop was sold in 1969.

PAINSWICK CHURCH, STRUCK BY LIGHTNING, 10 JUNE 1883. On the Sunday afternoon in question, a terrific thunderstorm struck the town. As the Stroud Journal reported, 'Soon after 5 o'clock a more than usually vivid flash, followed by an immediate and deafening roar, intimated that damage had been done and beholders were terrified to see the spire of the church fall with a crash.' A large portion of it fell through the church roof and, had it happened an hour later, many of the congregation would certainly have been killed. The hands of the clock on the tower stopped at eight minutes past five. Miraculously, not a single pane of stained glass was broken, though pews, prayer books and footstools were reduced to small pieces. Stones were scattered around the graveyard and some were hurled as far as the Falcon Hotel. Interestingly, a Mr Hanks, standing cutting lettuce at his door, had the knife twisted out of his hand, which was scorched and injured. The photograph is faded, but the hole in the nave roof is clearly visible.

THE CHURCH, *c.* 1850. Taken from an early Victorian print, this postcard shows the centre of the town before the demolition, in 1881, of the buildings on the left of New Street. No photograph of these premises is known. Before its removal in 1840, Painswick's first Town Hall stood behind the railings beyond the dog.

THE CLIPPING SERVICE, 1905. The Clipping Service has always taken place on the first Sunday after 19 September. 'Clipping' is derived from a Saxon word and means 'to encircle'. In this ceremony, which still thrives today, the church is completely surrounded by parishioners holding hands. A sermon is then preached in the graveyard. Here the Revd A.H.Stanton is seen delivering his address from the traditional location, the external steps on the north side of the building.

EDWARDIAN CROWD SCENE, CLIPPING SERVICE. Dressed in their Sunday best, townspeople stand in the churchyard, listening to an address delivered from the steps shown in the previous photograph. (The occasion may actually be the same.) Note the presence of the local police and fire brigade.

CLIPPING SERVICE, 1930s. Miss Drewitt (centre), in front of the banner, escorts a new generation of schoolchildren.

GENERAL BOOTH VISITS PAINSWICK. The founder of the Salvation Army, by this time an old man, paid a visit to Painswick in 1906. He is seen here in the centre of the town, standing in an early motor car, addressing a large crowd. General Booth was greeted by the Revd F.W. Brown, Minister of Painswick Congregational Church. The daughter of Edward Reed, a local manufacturer, gave him a bouquet, after which the General spoke about his life's work. He was a firm believer in vegetarianism and the Stroud News printed in full his recipe for 'a mid-day soup'.

THE TOWN HALL, c. 1926. This excellent photograph clearly shows the former position of the Victoria Jubilee Lamp, which was for so long a focal point in the town. 'Meet you at the lamp' was an often-heard phrase. (See page 33.)

THE WEMYSS MEMORIAL. The view shown here is interesting since it pre-dates the growth of much of the yew hedging now found in the gardens. Dated 4 October 1932, the postcard from which it is taken reads, 'Visited Painswick Church and this memorial with Amelia in her car. Tea at the King William Hotel, Birdlip, and called at the Sanatorium to see Tom.' Prior to 1921 Wellingtonia trees covered this piece of land, which was commonly known as Jumbo's Den, a favourite play haunt for the youth of the town. The memorial erected in 1930 commemorates the Misses Harriet and Alice Wemyss, who lived at Washwell House and who, as the inscription records, 'loved this parish for over 50 years, doing many acts of kindness to man, bird and beast.' Carved onto the side panels of the memorial are a working horse, poultry, cattle, dogs, birds and – charmingly – the Misses Wemyss' cockatoo!

MILK DELIVERY, 1920s. Accompanied by local children, Mr Frederick Webb is seen here in his milk delivery cart, pulled by Queenie. When this picture was taken one could still park a vehicle at right angles in the road with impunity.

EDWARDIAN EMPIRE DAY CELEBRATIONS, 1905. Here a group of schoolchildren pose in front of the Town Hall. They are wearing and carrying flowers and represent various parts of the Empire. Miss Maria Kirkland, for many years Headmistress of the Girls' School, stands next to the clergyman. What purpose the black object in the foreground serves is uncertain. Julian Slade, of Salad Days fame, lived with his family in the cottage on the right, 'St Michael's'.

EMPIRE DAY CELEBRATIONS SCENE, c. 1904. In this photograph a much larger group of children – presumably the entire Girls' School – can be seen. The lady on the far left is again Miss Kirkland.

THE STOCKS, *c.* 1912. This charming photograph shows village children grouped around the unusual 17th-century metal stocks, which still remain one of Painswick's tourist sights. The boy in the stocks is Jack Musgrove, who later ran a motor cycle repair business in New Street. (See pages 12, 36 and 41.)

THE STOCKS, *c.* 1927. In this later view Jim Ryland poses for photographer William Adams. Note the boy's stout hob-nailed boots, regulation wear at the period.

FRIDAY STREET. This picture, taken from a postcard of around 1910, typifies the rural tranquillity of Edwardian Painswick. In 1941, however, matters were entirely different. Shortly after 1 a.m. on 15 June the town was hit by a series of eight German bombs, one of which fell on the Bell Inn. In the raid several other buildings were hit, including properties in Tibbiwell and Poultry Court. Two people – both, ironically, evacuees – were killed.

Friday Street
Painswick, Glos.

MONTAGUE
RIVERS
'45

Above: MONTAGUE RIVERS, ARTIST. Montague Rivers seems to have arrived in Painswick in the early 1930s and, at first, lodged with a family called Beard in the centre of the town. At a later period he bought the house named Camperdown at Bulls Cross. He was a gifted artist and ink drawings, such as this one dated 1945, together with many charming water colours, survive from his artistic output. Montague Rivers was a strict vegetarian. His wife, Marie, gave singing lessons.

Right: CATHOLIC CHURCH, c. 1936. Its interior considerably altered today, Painswick Catholic church was, according to the writer of this postcard, 'A slaughter-house, transformed into a chapel by Miss Alice Howard, daughter of the Ambassador to the Holy See.' Born in 1876, Alice was a tireless worker for the Catholic cause in Painswick. Soon after her arrival in the district in 1921, she started to search for a building to convert into a church. In 1922 she purchased 16th-century Hale Cottage, where Mass was occasionally celebrated. As more of her Catholic friends settled near Painswick, Alice's quest for larger premises became more pressing, and in 1931 she acquired the present site, then owned by Mr Harris, a butcher. The chapel was completed by 1934 when it was blessed, on 15 August, by the Bishop of Clifton. Damaged by enemy action in 1941, the church was unusable for some years until its reopening on 19 February 1956.

THE CROSS, *c.* 1920. On the extreme left is Lizzie Clark's shop, where everything from paraffin to sweets could be bought. Beyond it is Reuben Harris' butcher's premises (earlier Webb's). In 1941 it was occupied by Herbert Ireland, who ran it as a newsagent's. It was destroyed in the German air-raid described earlier. Mrs Peggy Perrins, Mr Ireland's daughter, clearly remembers, after the bomb dropped, stumbling around the house, jumping into her wellingtons, putting on a fur coat and grabbing the shop cash box. She also recalls how the smell of cordite from the explosion mingled with the aroma from broken home-made wine casks! The family lived for some time afterwards in a converted poultry house that Mr Ireland acquired.

LAYING THE FOUNDATION STONE OF THE NURSES' HOME. This took place on Coronation Day, 2 June 1953, and was performed by Lady Weld-Forester, President of the Gloucestershire Nursing Association. The little girl presenting flowers to her is Janet Musty. C.W. Orr, the composer, stands to the right, in front of the wall.

TIBBIWELL STREET, c. 1930. The building on the extreme right, the Public Baths, was erected in 1924, following the demolition of the Malthouse. Opposite the Golden Heart are the double doors belonging to its stables, converted by Smith Bros. into a private house some years ago. Behind the line of boys are Mr Dodd's motorcycle and sidecar, which he later exchanged for a Singer saloon.

ARRESTED! In the mid-1920s an episode took place which has remained fixed in the memory of many older Painswick residents. Five young men, in a stolen car, broke into Horne's garage to acquire petrol. Detected and chased by police, they sped off towards Stroud. However, just as they were leaving Painswick at Lullingworth corner, they failed to negotiate the sharp bend and left the road. Two were killed. The main photograph shows the surviving trio under police arrest. The inset is of the damaged vehicle.

BISLEY STREET. Properties on the right side of the street have been considerably altered since this photograph was taken *c.* 1930. The sign for Rowland Smith's butcher's shop can be seen on the left, part way down the street. The garden, near left, was owned by a Mr Andrews before Mr Horne developed it as a garage. On one memorable occasion, a car travelling too fast down Cheltenham Road went through the garage and ended up suspended across the top of the retaining wall.

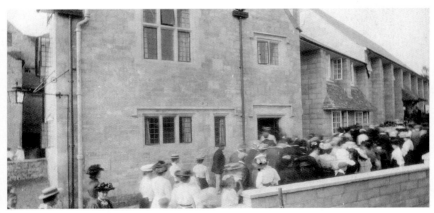

THE OPENING OF PAINSWICK INSTITUTE, SEPTEMBER 1907. The Institute was presented to the town by Mrs Frances Williams, of Gwynfa, now the Painswick Hotel. She was the mother-in-law of the Revd W. H. Seddon, Vicar of Painswick. It was built by the local firm of Burdock and Son. Lamps at the entrance were by Edward Gimson of Sapperton and Eric Gill was commissioned to carve an inscription. The Institute comprised a concert hall, billiard room, club room, library and green room – facilities still much utilised by the town.

VICARAGE STREET, c. 1910. Children crowd the foreground in this delightful study. Note the girls' bonnets. Down the street on the right a lady stands in the doorway of Frank Swain's chimney-sweeping business.

THE FALCON BOWLING GREEN, c. 1935. This ancient green claims to be the oldest in England. A plaque in the new Club House records that 'Between 1554 and 1803 the Jerninghams were Lords of Painswick Manor and here they placed the original Inn, together with Cock-Pit and Bowling Green, giving it for sign their Crest, the Falcon.' In 1731 a cock-fighting match is recorded between 'The Gentlemen of Painswick' and 'The Gentlemen of Stroud' involving no less than twenty-four birds.

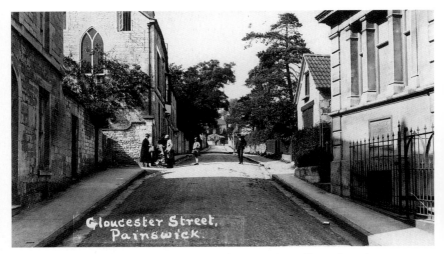

GLOUCESTER STREET, *c.* 1930. Taken by Stroud photographer William Adams, this view shows the Congregational Chapel, seen on the right. Founded in the 17th century and restored in 1892, its first minister was the Revd Francis Harris, who began his pastorate in 1672. The chapel is well-known for its stained glass window, designed by Burne-Jones and made in the William Morris workshops.

THE SANATORIUM, *c.* 1910. Not to be confused with the larger institution at Cranham, this sanatorium was run by Dr William McCall. Situated at The Croft, it has long since disappeared.

PAINSWICK HOUSE. Once known as Buenos Ayres, this fine house was built in the 1730s by Charles Hyett. His descendants, William Henry and Francis Adams Hyett, both took an active role in local and county affairs. Here the Painswick Parish Council Fire Brigade is seen practising at the house in 1896. Mr Hyett's daughter agreed to be 'rescued'.

THE SNOWDROP GROVE. The impressive Painswick House Rococo Gardens, which date from the mid-18th century, are of national importance and include a large collection of snowdrops. As the picture indicates, early spring visits to this beauty spot were already popular in Edwardian days.

PAINSWICK BEACON, c. 1930. The interest here lies in the absence of the trees which now cover so much of this part of the Beacon. Note the small boy to the right.

MOTORING, c. 1911. The reverse side of this postcard is stamped 'Greetings from Reginald C. Hill', so it is fair to assume that at least one of the motorists shown is a member of that family. The location is Painswick Cemetery. The vehicle is thought to be a Peugeot, made c. 1903-4 and registered in St Helens.

HOME FARM, PAINSWICK. This farm, later known as Hill Farm, was closest to Painswick House, hence its name. In the centre of the picture it is just possible to see a steam traction-engine and a threshing machine covered with a tarpaulin bearing the name of S. Berry, Holcombe Farm. Possibly the two farms were worked together in this period.

WASHWELL HOUSE. The Misses Wemyss lived here in 1907 when this photograph was taken. Note the unmetalled road and the extensive ivy covering the buildings. At a later period it is recalled that the Wemyss sisters kept a white cockatoo in a cage by a window on the left of the building. When passing youngsters jumped up and down in front of it, the bird would mimic them. This was regular Sunday entertainment for Painswick children.

PARADISE, 1899. The white building in the centre of the picture is the appropriately named Adam and Eve Inn, now closed. Beech trees prevent it from being seen from this viewpoint today. The figure on the right is Oscar Owers and the photograph is believed to have been taken by his wife. Mr Owers ran a photography business in Southsea. Following his marriage to Winifred Watkins, a local girl, he took an extensive series of fine pictures of the area in 1899.

ADAM AND EVE INN, PARADISE. Outside the public house a group of local people pause to watch the photographer. A horse and cart has pulled up in the roadway. The date of the picture is around 1910.

THE PARK, c. 1925. The interest in this picture lies in the absence of the buildings which have since sprung up on the site.

AN EDWARDIAN CYCLIST. This photograph was taken outside Kings Mill House in the summer of 1907. It belongs with the picture of the motor car at Painswick Cemetery (see page 28). The photograph either shows, or was taken by, Reginald C. Hill. There is reason to believe that the Hill family owned or rented Kings Mill House.

THE STROUD TO PAINSWICK MOTOR BUS. A motor bus service was inaugurated between Painswick and Stroud in January 1905 by the Great Western Railway Company. On the Saturday prior to the official opening day a trial run was made with a pair of buses carrying dignitaries from the two towns. On arrival at Painswick an excellent luncheon was taken at the Falcon, followed by speeches. In one of these Mr St Clair Baddeley amusingly referred to his 'Jacob's Ladder Dream' in which, instead of angels ascending a ladder to Heaven, he saw motor buses going up and down the hill to Painswick! After the festivities in the Falcon concluded, the party returned to Stroud. The Milnes Daimler buses seated 22 passengers, could carry 15 cwt of luggage and were powered by 20 h.p. engines. In the upper picture a motor bus arrives by rail at Stroud Station. The lower view shows the route's terminus at the Falcon Hotel, Painswick.

THE MOTOR BUS AT THE JUBILEE LAMP. Franked on 26 January 1905, this postcard shows the motor bus at Painswick, probably on its maiden run. The lamp was erected in 1904 (somewhat belatedly) 'to commemorate the completion of the sixtieth year of the reign of Her Most Gracious Majesty, the late Queen Victoria, by the loyal inhabitants of Painswick, in token of their thankfulness that a reign so beneficent should have been so prolonged.' The railings have now gone and the lamp has been repositioned.

SETTING OFF FOR STROUD. Here a smaller motor bus sets out from Beacon House. Mr Herbert Ireland stands on the left and Mrs Westcott, whose family ran the Falcon Hotel, is seated at the front, next to the postman.

GYPSY RYLES. Walter Ryles, described in the Stroud press as 'King of the Gypsies', lived alone in his caravan at Hillfoot. A kindly and genial man, conspicuous by his long wavy grey hair, he was in increasingly frail health as 1905 began, and local children were sent up with hot tea for him. On 1 February he failed to respond to their calls. One of the Stroud Guardians was summoned and discovered him dead. Gypsy Ryles had been a familiar sight around the town in all weathers. His age was estimated at between 70 and 80. A large number of gypsies attended his funeral.

BROTHER MICHAEL. A familiar and well-loved local character, Brother Michael, whose real name was John Doe, lived in a room over the Lych Gate at the western end of the churchyard and acted as assistant to various Painswick vicars. He also enjoyed working an allotment in Kemps Lane. Brother Michael died in November 1962 at the age of 90.

PAINSWICK FIRE BRIGADE, *c.* 1900. The town's horse-drawn fire-engine is seen here with its crew. The location of the picture is thought to be Cheltenham Road. Walter H. Burdock is the officer on the right. On the left, next to the policeman, is his son Frederick. Members of the Fern, Tidmarsh and Ryland families are also known to be present.

PAINSWICK RETAINED FIREMEN, 1945. They are, left to right, back row: Frank Price, Frank Workman, Ken Archard, Ivan Dodd. Front row: Ned Tranter, Frank Cooke, Bob Gardiner, Cyril Hogg, Jack Musgrove. (The last mentioned is the person seen on page 12 standing by his cycle repair shop, on page 19 in the stocks and in the Painswick football team on page 41.)

THE PRIMITIVE METHODIST ELDERS. Photographed around 1890, these venerable gentlemen are described as 'Three elders of the Primitive Methodist Chapel in Painswick'. They are, from left to right, Joseph Woodfield, Thomas Spring and William Clissold. The last named died on 28 November 1893 at the age of 73.

PAINSWICK BOYS' SCHOOL, c. 1930. Mr Slack (right) was evidently a schoolmaster who ruled with a rod of iron, as many stories concerning his methods of enforcing discipline testify. The group shown is, left to right, front row: A. Parkes, G. Partridge, Miss K. Moody, J. Bowles, T. Hollister. Second row: C. Garner, ? Allen, ? Dunn, N. Faulkner, A. Walker, C. Foxwell, B. Walklett. Third row: F. Spring, E. Daniels, H. Arch, T. Berry, ? Hindmarsh, F. Kilminster. Back row: W. Beeson, ? Grisewood, B. Snow, J. Groves.

PAINSWICK GIRLS' SCHOOL OUTING, *c.* 1910. Before the First World War a trip to Stroud was considered a reasonable treat. Here the children are seen in Kendrick Street. Most appear to have travelled the three miles or so in a farm wagon, though an older pupil seems to have used her bicycle.

PAINSWICK GIRLS' SCHOOL, *c.* 1925. Those pictured are, left to right, back row: Ruby Hogg, Ivy Ryland, Lilian Clack, -?-, Phyllis Cocklin, Ethel Musty. In front of them are Miss Arnold, Betty King, ? Cox, Betty Wilkins, Irene Perrin. Seated: Miss Kirkland, Pearl Parsons, Peggy Ireland, Joan Millard, Nellie Tipping, Kathleen Ireland, May Musty, Miss Butler. On the ground: Elsie Barnfield, Edith Gyde, Mary Gerrish, ? Gibb.

PAINSWICK GIRLS' SCHOOL, c. 1929-30. Here can be seen, left to right, front row: Rona Jones, Pearl Parsons, Joan Merchant, Diana Webb, ? Georgina Packer, Stella Birt. Second row: Barbara Wright, Martha Lawrence, Irene Gardiner, Miss Kirkland, Miss Butler, Joan Ireland, Betty Mason, Miss Murray. Third row: -?-, -?-, Ivy Ryland, Irene Perrins, Nancy Merchant, -?-, Kathleen Miles, Eva West, Kathleen Ireland. Back row: Lena Birt, Violet Beale, Betty Wilkins, Ivy Spring, ? Nellie Tipping, Lilian Woodman, Leonora Nurse.

PAINSWICK INFANTS' SCHOOL, DECEMBER 1932. Left to right, front row: -?-, Jean Bayliss, ? Hatton, Joan Barnard, Alfred Kilminster, Edward Gyde, Stanley Woodham, Doreen Thornton, ? Jack Smith, Marjorie Ireland, Tony Cook, Eric Bullingham. Second row: Tony Birt, Peter Bollen, Harold Pearce, -?-, Grace Gyde, -?-, ? Bullingham, -?-, Joyce Bridgeman, Hugh Cornock, -?-, Joyce Musgrove, Kathleen Jones. Back row: ? Geoff Smith, ? Bertie Smith, Charlie Spring, Tony Bushell, Tony Smart, Kathleen Mansell, Lilian Dee, June Lamort, -?-, Geoff Simmonds, Beattie Foxwell, Ken Mills. The teachers are Miss Toft and Miss Owen.

PAINSWICK ASSOCIATION FOOTBALL TEAM, 1913-1914 SEASON. Left to right, back row: Miss Seddon, T. Musgrove (with a mascot (?) on his shoulder), E. Duxbury, A. Smith, B. Duxbury, P. Lewis, Miss Cooke. Middle row: W. Birt, D. Cooke (vice capt.), J. Musgrove (capt.), O. Manns, E. Tranter. Front row: A. Swain, F. Bridgeman.

PAINSWICK RUGBY CLUB, 1930-1931 SEASON. This photograph shows the team that won the Mid-Glos. Rugby Cup. They are, left to right, front row: P. Bridgeman (Hon. Sec.), B. Perrins, E. Musty, J. Musty, S. Gyde, E. Luker, Sam Gyde (trainer). Second row: T.G. Goddard (Chairman), C. Hogg, C.A. Launder, R. Bridgeman (Captain), C.F. Webb, W. Birt, I. Dodd, H. Tranter (Committee). Back row: W. Tranter (Hon. Treasurer), P. Ireland (Groundsman), D. Barnard, G. Fry, T. Turner, B. Meadows, L. Ryland, F. Jones (Committee), R. Musty (Committee).

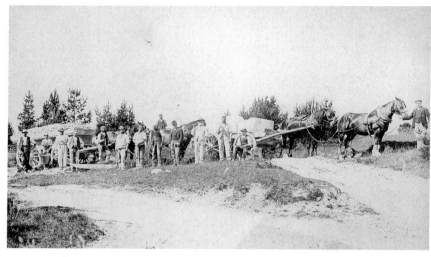

STONE QUARRYING, PAINSWICK BEACON, *c.* 1900. Quarrying has been carried out at Painswick for many generations, as is evident from the numerous fine Cotswold stone buildings in the town. This important picture is thought to date from around the turn of the century and to have been taken at the point where the metalled road now crosses a ridge near Catbrain Quarry. Note the large saw used for cutting the limestone blocks (left foreground).

THE WEBB FAMILY HAYMAKING. The Webbs are seen here haymaking at Hambutts Orchard, opposite Dryknapps Field. On top of the stack is Frederick Webb. His son Cuthbert is on the right with Ernest Griffiths next to him. The horse was called Tom.

THE ANCIENT SOCIETY OF PAINSWICK YOUTHS. The title of this group of Painswick bellringers is undeniably quaint. Ancient it most certainly is – in 1986 its tercentenary was celebrated. The term 'youths' is more open to question, as the photograph demonstrates. Here we see the members following their record peal of 13,001 Changes, which lasted 8 hours 45 minutes and took place on 14 February 1920. The ringers are, left to right, back row: J. Ballinger, F. Cole, A.E. Wright (Master), A. Hanks, C. Austin. Seated: T. Baldwin, C. Gardener, H. Scrivens, A. Hannis, W. Hastings, W. Staite. On the ground: W. Ireland.

THE HISTORICAL PAG-EANT OF 1911. Held at Fromehall Park in Stroud, the Mid-Gloucestershire Historical Pageant of Progress attempted to record what its author, Frank Gwynne Evans, considered the more imp-ortant episodes of English history as they affected this area. Hundreds of local people took part and different episodes were allocated to various towns and villages. Painswick helped to represent the Civil War period of the mid-17th Century. Here are seen two splendidly costumed Painswick participants, Maurice Cooke as Colonel Massey, with his daughter Edith (who later married Jack Musgrove) as a Puritan Maid.

FEEDING THE PIGS. Photographed sometime between the Wars, Albert and Eliza Musty stand outside their door at Forge Cottage, Butt Green.

THE PAINSWICK BANNER. Now lost, the celebrated Painswick banner, which featured so prominently in the town's social life a century ago, represented many colourful aspects of its history: a church bell and a handbell; the weathervane so famously used for target practice; the parapet of the church tower; a yew tree; Churchwardens' pipes; a pawnbroker's sign (to represent the poverty of many Painswick people at the period); a quart cider mug; the stocks and, most importantly, Bow-Wow Pie – containing dog meat and served, it is claimed, to visitors from Stroud instead of a more traditional filling! The men on either side of the banner probably represented the characters in the poem 'The Three Old Men of Painswick,' whose extreme longevity was supposedly attributable to the town's healthy air. (Incidentally, some families today still celebrate the anniversary of Painswick Feast Day with a pie in which is concealed a small china dog. The finder is entitled to be called 'Honorary Bow-Wow!')

IN FESTIVE MOOD. At Christmas 1912 Painswick scholars certainly appear to have enjoyed dressing up, though whether for a play or a fancy dress competition is not recorded. The girl on the left, in Scottish costume, is Chrissie Cook. Slightly to the right behind her is Melville Ireland. Third from the right on the front row is Irene Ireland. Marjorie Tidmarsh is on the extreme right, wearing a large hat.

OPEN-AIR DRAMA AT PAINSWICK HOUSE. This photograph shows a play called The Prince who was a Piper taking place in the Rococo Garden c. 1946/7. Such productions were supported and organised by Miss Lucy Hyett, who lived at the house. The character on the left is Julian Slade, who spent many years in Painswick and was, of course, famous as the composer of Salad Days.

THE CORONATION PAGEANT, 1953. Harold Mason, of Dell Farm, Sheepscombe, provided a tractor and trailer to draw the Painswick Amateur Operatic Society's Carnival Float, 'Cinderella'. On it are seen, at the back, Faith West and Peter Boulton. In front, Pauline Webb is between Bill Wexham and (right) her brother, Cuthbert Webb. Jean Hughes is kneeling in front.

THE GONDOLIERS, FEBRUARY 1952. Staged by the Operatic Society in the Institute, The Gondoliers was one of a series of successful shows the company produced in the post-war years. Seen here are Casilda, left, (Margaret Young) with her page, Clare Webb, and the Duchess of Plaza-Toro (Ruby Harper) with her page, Bill Perrins.

MILK DELIVERY. Philip Monk sets off on his rounds. He was born at Paradise in 1892, married at Painswick in 1913, and fought in the First World War. Philip, who worked for the Berry family for many years as a farm labourer, lived most of his life in a cottage by the Institute and died in 1965.

Two

Sheepscombe

SHEEPSCOMBE, GENERAL VIEW. The village church must be one of the most distinctive in the country, though it cannot be said that the design of its tower has always met with universal approval. This fine early view of the parish is by the photographer Paul Smith and must date from before 1872, when the south aisle of the church was built. It is also interesting to note at least three buildings which had gone by the turn of the century.

THE CHURCH OF SAINT JOHN THE APOSTLE. The foundation stone of Sheepscombe church was laid in 1819 and the building was consecrated on 21 February 1820. The Revd Neville was its first vicar. This view of the interior, dating from around 1900, shows the choir stalls before they were moved into the south aisle. Electric lighting had not then, of course, been installed. The boards on either side of the chancel arch contained the Lord's Prayer and the Ten Commandments.

IN A COTTAGE GARDEN, *c.* 1930. Eva Herbert and Sam Foxwell stand by a fine display of lilies in the garden of what is now known as Myrtle Cottage. Running unseen between the garden and the church is the road.

THE JACKSONS' PONY. Here, *c.* 1904, Eva Jackson (1900-1965) enjoys a ride on the family pony, assisted by her mother, Maud, who appears again on the following page. Apart from alterations to the leading of its windows, the church beyond remains relatively unchanged.

THE VILLAGE, *c.* 1910. Centre right can be seen the stream which is shown in the introduction to this book, together with the cottages that, around 1927, were converted into the Village Hall. Just to the left of the road is the building which then housed the village post office, run for many years by Agnes Partridge, who also operated a laundry. This view of Sheepscombe is now partially obscured by several large trees.

Above: VIEW FROM ABOVE CYPRUS COTTAGE. The cottage in the immediate foreground is aptly named 'Endways.' Beyond it is Cyprus Cottage, built by the Partridge family. Across the road, tombstones in the upper section of the graveyard can be glimpsed.

Left: MAUD JACKSON. Seen here near Jack's Green in 1937, when she was in her late seventies, is Maud Jackson, who kept a cow – though on this occasion it is possible that she is carrying water rather than milk. She lived at Laburnum Cottage.

FORTUNE'S WELL. Converted from a row of cottages as a retreat by the Theosophical Society in the 1920s, these premises were acquired in 1932 by a Mr and Mrs Rogers and re-opened as a vegetarian boarding establishment under the title of the Food Reform Guest House of the Cotswolds. Mr Rogers, it is remembered, invariably wore shorts, whatever the climate or season. The projecting annexe nearest to camera was the new dining room built for the Rogers by Freeman and Son of Camp.

CELEBRATIONS FOR THE RELIEF OF MAFEKING. In May 1900 Sheepscombe school-children celebrated the ending of the 217-day Siege of Mafeking, one of the most notable events of the Boer War. National flags in the playground seem entirely appropriate, though what purpose the tin bath served is unclear!

THE SCHOOL PLAYGROUND, c. 1902. Note that, a century or so ago, caps were de rigueur when attending school, though jackets might be removed when play became particularly frenzied. The boys are, left to right, -?-, Bill Boulton, Percy Crosswell, Walter Fern, -?-, Lewis Sollars and George Fern, all born between 1890 and 1892.

BROOKLANDS POND, c. 1903. This was the pond serving the mill, closed in 1839, belonging to John Wight, a considerable benefactor of the parish back in the 1820s when the church was built. The small girl in the foreground is Carmen Maurice and her story is fascinating. She was born in Russia. Her mother, married to a general who was not Carmen's father and not kindly disposed towards the child, taught the children of Leo Tolstoy. He advised her to escape to England, which she did, settling at Whiteway Colony, where Carmen was apparently left, aged about 18 months. Her mother later returned and took her to Paris, where she grew up and studied music. She became a composer and eventually settled in Canada.

SCHOOL GROUP, c. 1931. At this period children remained at Sheepscombe School only up to the age of 9, when they transferred to Painswick. The pupils are, left to right, back row: Eva Herbert, Sylvia Cox, Marion Light, Margaret Partridge, Noelle Holder, Beryl Fern, Marjorie Hemming. Middle row: Dora Lambert, Arthur Herbert, Peter Brown, John Wescombe, John Plumb, Beryl Hemming, Ted Holford, Alan Smith. Seated: Neville West, Fay West, Betty Brown, Barrie Merrett, Pat Plumb.

EVACUEES GARDENING. Many Stroud area evacuees came from Clacton-on-Sea in Essex, including several of those shown here, busy on land just below the school in the early years of the Second World War. Among those names recalled are Fred Carr, Madeline Morris, Mary Reed, Kenny Jones, Beryl Bates, Stanley Page, Tony Smith and Rose Eagle.

A CIRCUS AT BRIAR COTTAGE, 1940s. Briar Cottage, just above the Village Hall, was owned for many years by the Misses Turquand who, purely as a hobby, involved local children in amateur dramatic productions. The circus cast are, left to right, standing: Stella Rand, Violet Holder, -?-, Evelyn Statham, Doreen Wilson, Maureen Skevall. Front row: Joy Sollars, Marguerite Statham, -?-, John Eveleigh.

DEDICATION OF THE WAR MEMORIAL, 1921. The designer of the cross was W. St Clair Baddeley of Painswick. The memorial was unveiled by Maj.-Gen. Sir L.V. Swaine, KCB, CMG, after which it was dedicated by the Revd K.K.E. Richards. This ceremony followed a procession which started from the school, consisting of children, ex-servicemen and the Sheepscombe Band, who played 'Soldiers of the Cross.'

THE VILLAGE SHOP. Housed in converted farm buildings attached to Briar Cottage, the village shop and post office, run for many years by Mr and Mrs Horace Brown (the latter seen here) finally closed in the mid-1980s. Like all such establishments, it evidently stocked a wide range of items.

TWO-WHEELED TRANSPORT. In this photograph of c. 1902, two ladies, who may be members of the Jackson family, linger by Laburnum Cottage at Jack's Green. Their splendid Edwardian hats were, of course, considered necessary attire for any outing.

SHEEPSCOMBE WOMEN'S INSTITUTE. This photograph was taken at a Gloucestershire Federation gathering at Badminton on 20 July 1922. The ladies shown are, left to right, back row: A. Green, E. Jackson, Mrs Crosswell, E. Workman, F. Green. Middle row: Mrs Canton, Mrs Snow, Mrs F. Sollars, Mabel Sollars, Mrs Herbert, Mrs West. Front row: Mrs Pratt, Mrs Plumb, Mrs Sollars, Mrs Bullock, Mrs Hanson (President), Mrs Messenger (Treasurer), Mrs Jolly (Secretary), Mrs L. Hogg, Mrs L. Sollars.

THE PLOUGH INN. This view of some festive occasion outside The Plough Inn, situated on the main road near the present-day bus stop, is an interesting one. It is probably connected with electioneering, since the banners relate to the Conservative Party and several people are wearing rosettes. It is possible that the picture dates from the run-up to the 1900 General Election, when Charles Allen, Liberal, polled 4,692 votes in the Stroud Constituency, narrowly defeating C.A. Cripps, Conservative, by 313 votes.

THE HORSE-POWERED CIDER MILL. Run by the Workman family – Walter (left) and Ernest are in the lower picture – this cider mill closed in the 1940s. The upper view shows fruit crushing and the lower one the cider press. The Workman family still occupy these premises, now unsurprisingly named 'The Cider House'.

CORONATION CELEBRATIONS, 1902. Pictured here in Jubilee Field, near Magpie Bottom, are, left to right, back row: Albert Sollars, George Sollars, the bailiff from Lodge Farm (?), Jack Light, Ernest Workman and Sam Sollars. Front row: Sid Barnett the postman, Arthur Halliday, William Hogg, Fred Sparrow and David Heyden. The boy is Eddie Smith.

AN OUTING. The girl seated at the very front of the decorated wagon is believed to be Annie Green, born in 1899. From her apparent age it is deduced that the photograph probably shows part of George V's Coronation celebrations in 1911. Mrs Jolly, wife of George Jolly, headmaster of the village school, is also sitting at the front of the wagon, which belonged to Henry Boulton. Albert Sollars stands below, behind the horse. The picture is taken near The Butcher's Arms.

THE VILLAGE WHEELWRIGHT'S SHOP. Samuel Scott, founder of the family wheel-wright's business, was born around 1817. He opened his business in the 1860s and it ran through to the 1950s, when the lower picture was taken. In it Gilbert Scott is seen making final adjustments to a vehicle ordered, curiously, for a farmer at Maidenhead. The upper photograph is of the exterior of the workshop itself.

TILLING WITH A BREASTPLOUGH. In this splendid and important picture of what, by Edwardian days, must already have been an archaic method of preparing the soil, Charles Sollars works his garden at Honeysuckle Cottage. The house, now called Greycot, is in the background. Charles died in 1922 at the age of 65.

HARVESTING THE HAY. This fine photograph must date from around 1910 and was taken in Croft Field in the centre of the village. In the mid-1980s three houses were built in the field. Honeysuckle Cottage and School House are among the buildings visible in the background.

MILK DELIVERY, DELL FARM. The date of this photograph is unknown, but it was probably taken between the Wars.

CUTTING THE CORN. These atmospheric photographs, also taken at Dell Farm, show a reaper-binder at work. From the 1930s through to the 1950s the farm was worked by the Mason family.

Three

Slad

SLAD, GENERAL VIEW. Taken around 1890, probably by Nailsworth photographer Paul Smith, this peaceful view of Slad is easily recognisable today, as so little housing development has since taken place.

SLAD CONGREGATIONAL CHAPEL. The chapel (closed in the mid-1970s) is now a guest house and considerably altered. When this photograph was taken, a burial had clearly just occurred though, rather oddly, the flowers seem to have been placed on planking over the open grave, rather than on the soil when it had been filled. The chapel foundation stone was laid in 1865.

THE STAR INN, THE VATCH. In this atmospheric view, dating from around the turn of the century, a carter pauses in the road near The Star public house. The landlord at the time was Henry Mitchell.

THE CENTRE OF THE VILLAGE, 1920s. This scene on the main road through Slad remains largely unchanged today, though F.J. Brown's building firm has long ceased to be run from the premises on the right. Just out of sight to the left is the childhood home of Laurie Lee, whose youngest brother Tony, according to several local people, is one of the small boys sitting on the bank.

SLAD SCHOOL, 1920s. This charming photograph shows the school as it was at the period so evocatively portrayed in Cider with Rosie. The headmistress, Miss Wardley, stands by the wall at the bottom of the picture.

SLAD SCHOOLCHILDREN, c. 1923. Left to right, back row: ? Ernie Smith, -?-, -?-, ? Bill Fern, Wilson Twinning, ? Cecil Smart, ? Ernie Smart. Middle row: Ernie Gleed, Freda Attwood, Eileen Brown, Louie Davis, Betty Gleed, -?-, Alice Green, May Twinning. Front row: Jim Fern, Florrie Attwood, Christine Blackwell, ? Doreen Brown, Clarice Hogg, Winnie Smart, ? Victor Smart, Beryl Twinning, -?-.

THE BIRD AND TREE COMPETITION, c. 1920. The shield displayed here was awarded for a nature study project in which pupils were required to write essays on their chosen bird and tree. Medals were also given, as can be seen in the photograph. (In Cider with Rosie Laurie Lee refers to being given medals for his faked compositions on the lives and habits of otters.) Those standing are, left to right, Miss Wardley, Bill Timbrell, Eva Lasbury, Percy Davis, Annie Timbrell. Seated are Archie Gleed and Harold Robinson.

VILLAGE CHILDREN, EARLY 1920s. This photograph is also set very much in the Cider with Rosie period. Amongst those identified are Annie Timbrell, Eva and ? Sydney Lasbury, Archie Gleed, Harold and Kenneth Robinson, May Twinning, Percy Davis, Alice Green, Edna and Florrie Hopkins, Fred Green, Betty Gleed and, standing with hands clasped together, 'Rosie'.

KING GEORGE V'S SILVER JUBILEE, 1935. As part of the celebrations, a procession passes along the village street. In the middle distance is the Slad Jazz Band, led by its drum major, Mr Puttick. The tall man on the left at the front of the band is Jim Fern.

SLAD SCHOOLCHILDREN, c. 1937. At this period only children up to the age of eight attended Slad School, after which they transferred to Uplands. The children are, left to right, back row: Donald Halliday, Dorothy Davis, Marjorie Warner, Hubert Twinning, Barbara Tanner, John Eldridge. Middle row: Edgar Avery, Guy Grearson, Maureen Edwards, Barbara Thomas, Douglas Timbrell, ? Dorothy Smith, John Phillips. Front row: Dorothy Puttick, Claude Hearne, Pat and Jean Brookes, Margaret Hearne, Pat Ballinger.

THE GARDEN, STEANBRIDGE HOUSE. This view, taken around 1930, shows members of the Jones family relaxing in their extensive gardens at Steanbridge House. They are, left to right: Marian (née Oliphant, widow of Samuel Gilbert Jones who died in 1926), Isabel Ethel Jones, Dorothy Oliphant, Miss Cowen, and the Revd Walter Anthony Jones, of the Old House, brother of Samuel Gilbert, who lived to be 98.

CARNIVAL, STEANBRIDGE HOUSE. In the inter-war years many parish events took place at Steanbridge House. Here a carnival procession is seen near the main door. The conservatory attached to the building has survived, though the greenhouse in the distance has been rebuilt and reduced in size.

THE SUNDIAL, STEANBRIDGE HOUSE. This unusual structure, a feature of the garden, was later taken to another Jones family home, 'The Reddings' at Fretherne. It was subsequently moved to Worcestershire.

STEANBRIDGE HOUSE, INTERIOR VIEWS. In 1907, when these photographs were taken, Steanbridge House was owned by Samuel Gilbert Jones, portrayed so colourfully as the Squire in Cider with Rosie. Note the splendidly cluttered drawing room and, below, the dining room with a family portrait on the wall. Steanbridge House was built in Tudor or Jacobean times as a clothier's home and was much enlarged in the 19th century. The Townsend family owned it for many years.

THE BUNGALOWS, SLAD. Now known as 'Overdale' (nearest to the camera) and 'Little Orchard', these bungalows were built in the early 1920s on the top side of the main road leading to Bulls Cross. Note how clear of shrubs and trees the hillside then was. By an interesting coincidence, the author's grandfather, W.E. Beard, built 'Overdale', the original plans for which have survived.

A COTSWOLD COTTAGE, THE VATCH. This charming old property, now demolished, lay off the main road down a track opposite and a little further up the road from the old Star Inn. The occupants shown are, left to right, Mrs Victoria Hughes, her son Arthur and daughter Mabel (later Mrs Purvey).

ENTRANCE TO STEANBRIDGE LANE, *c.* 1910. In this peaceful rural photograph note the two small girls in the foreground, the trap in the distance and the trellised roses in the well-kept cottage garden on the left.

ELCOMBE. Of all the hamlets in the Stroud district, Elcombe must surely rank as one of the most secluded and attractive. This photograph was taken around 1908. Some cottages have been altered or extended since then, but Elcombe's charm remains largely unspoiled today. In the house nearest to camera lived 'Miss Flynn', whose suicide by drowning was described so graphically in Cider with Rosie and made such an impression on the young Laurie Lee.

VATCH MILL. It seems almost impossible that such a large industrial complex as this should have existed within the narrow confines of the Slad valley. Vatch Mill was operated in the 1830s by the Marling family. It contained several steam engines and power looms. The mill had become derelict by 1890 and was demolished soon afterwards, killing a bystander when the chimney stack fell. A red-brick cottage was built with materials from this chimney.

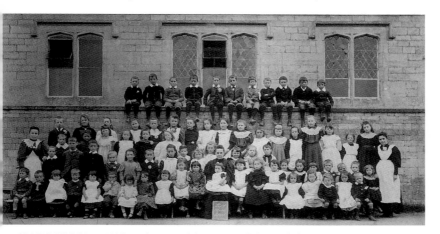

SLAD SCHOOL, c. 1895. At the turn of the century Slad provided a surprisingly large number of pupils for its village school, as this fine photograph proves. Notice the girls' aprons and the boys' starched collars. Cecil Fern is sixth from the left in the second row from the front. The school closed in 1968.

MILK DELIVERY. Here Mr Phillips, of Slad Dairy, is seen at the Vatch, filling a pail from his milk churn. At one period his business was run from Peghouse Farm. With him are his wife's sister and half-sister.

A CHARABANC OUTING TO CHEDDAR GORGE, LATE 1920s. Amongst those seated the following have been identified: Mrs Gardiner, Miss Restall, Beattie Davis, Gladys Thomas (with her young son Don), Fred Tilley, Ernest and Dot Vick, Leslie Gardiner and Mrs Vick.

CORONATION ARCH, THE VATCH, 1911. To celebrate both local and national events, arches were erected quite commonly in towns at this period. However, it is less usual to find them in rural locations. The Stroud Journal of 23 June 1911 proves, in fact, that this was one of four such arches built in Slad. On Coronation Day a children's procession assembled at the Vatch arch and proceeded through the village to the final arch, before arriving at Steanbridge House, where tea was provided for the children and a 'meat tea' for adults. Before dispersing, the youngsters were given souvenir boxes of chocolates and packets of sweets.

FIFTY YEARS ON. This pair of photographs shows the wedding of Jack Twinning and Matilda Hanks on 4 June 1910, and the same couple cutting their golden wedding cake at The Ridings in 1960.

Above: VATCH MILL COTTAGES. Here Hubert Twinning, son of Jack and Matilda, sits in front of his home – 3, Spring Cottages, The Vatch – together with Pat, the family dog. The building was formerly part of Vatch Mill offices.

Left: THE OLD SLAD HUT, 1933. The reception for the wedding of May, daughter of Jack and Matilda Twinning, to Clifford Hopkins took place in the old Slad Hut, which stood in Steanbridge Lane until just after the Second World War and was the venue for many village functions.

Four

Edge

THE POTATO PICKERS, *c.* 1910. This picture, taken at the junction of Sevenleaze Lane with the main Gloucester to Stroud road, is such a fine example of rural life that it would merit inclusion in any national collection. Left to right are Mr Marsh, Mr Partridge, and Mr Fluck standing behind his sons, Reg – with a posy of flowers – Wilfred and Charlie.

EDGE CHURCH. In 1866 St John the Baptist church was built. By 1927, when this photograph was taken, trees in the graveyard had had time to reach maturity. The vicar, Revd L.B. Cholmondeley, is seen here together with staff and pupils from the village school.

CHURCH INTERIOR, 1930s. The principal differences we would notice, comparing this picture with the church as it is today, are that the wall-paintings, hanging lamps and candle-sticks have all disappeared.

LOCALS AT THE 'GLOUCESTER HOUSE.' Dating from the 1920s, this postcard of locals at the Gloucester House, now renamed the Edgemoor Inn, is another photographic gem. The assembled company are, left to right, Mr Marsh (see page 79), Joe Fluck, Dan Marsh, George Birt, Bert King, Tom Newman (the licensee), Fred Fluck, Mr Bateman, George Fluck and Joe Peachey.

AN OUTING. Seen prior to departure from the Gloucester House in the 1920s are, left to right, front row: -?-, -?-, Vic Mills, George Birt, Charlie Fluck, -?-, Mr Tranter, Arthur Broderick, -?-, Tom Newman, Mr Bateman, Mr Tilling, Arthur Berry. Behind them are: -?-, Fred Fluck, an unknown boy, George Fluck, Bert King, Wilf Fluck, Mr Peachey, Joe Peachey, William Fluck, John Wright, Mr Cook. Oliver Birt is between the rows, in front of William Fluck.

ALLANHAY COTTAGE, STOCKEND. During the 1930s this was the home of writer and broadcaster C. Henry Warren, who wrote A Cotswold Year, an evocative description of Gloucestershire through the seasons. Into his book Warren put, under pseudonyms, many local people.

RUDGE HILL, c. 1920. This delightfully composed picture shows, left to right, Jessie Berry, Muriel Wright, Lily Andrews (clutching a small stool) and Mary Field. It must count as one of the most charming in the collection.

EDGE INSTITUTE, 1920s. Wooden buildings obviously have a limited lifespan and it is important that they are recorded. Edge Institute, constructed from First World War army huts, was erected around 1920, taken down in the 1980s and replaced by the present stone-built structure.

JENKINS FARM, c. 1910. This atmospheric photograph was acquired among a group of unidentified pictures, so it was pleasing to pinpoint its location.

EDGE SCHOOL, c. 1924. The teachers are Miss Archard, left, and Mrs Booth. The pupils have been identified as, left to right, front row: ? Sidney Holder, Derek Wood, Philip Peachey, Jack Wood, ? Holder, ? Holder, Ted White, ? Holder. Second row: Renee Edwards, Joyce Browning, ? Ractliffe, Dinky Burcombe, Pinky Ractliffe, Sybil Griffiths, Betty Ractliffe, Phyllis Edwards, Winnie Birt, Lily White, Lou Feltham. Third row: Trixie Feltham, Lilian Prout, Myrtle Guy, Winnie Fluck, Lena Cook, Nancy Parry, Nancy Edwards, Martha White, Muriel Wright, Nancy Vowles. Back row: Mary Feltham, Bill Griffiths, George World, Harold Butler, Lancelot Parry, Bertie Wood, Eddie Wathern, Charlie Broderick.

EDGE SCHOOL, EARLY 1930s. Space prevents naming all the youngsters shown in this later school photograph. The staff are Mrs Booth, left, and Miss Jefferies. In the centre is the Revd P.A. Hippisley-Smith.

MAYPOLE DANCING, EDGE HOUSE, 1920s. Miss Archard, left, and Mrs Booth supervise the group which comprises, left to right, back row: Muriel Wright, Myrtle Guy, Martha White, Nancy Edwards, Trixie Feltham, Nancy Parry, Lena Cook. Middle row: Renee Edwards, Lou Feltham, Joyce Browning, Nancy Vowles, Phyllis Edwards, Betty Ractliffe, Winnie Fluck. Front row: Bertie Wood, -?-, Pinky Ractliffe, Charlie Broderick, Derek Wood, Owen Feltham, Robert Tilling.

BLACKSMITH'S FORGE. This superb image is reputed to be of premises in Back Edge Lane, though there is some doubt as to its precise location. However, it is still thought worth including here as an outstanding example of a rural life photograph of a century or so ago. Note the circular stone platform for fixing metal tyres to cartwheels.

EDGE AND PITCHCOMBE FOOTBALL TEAM. The picture dates from the 1920s. In the back row are, left to right: Mr Barnfield, Mr Birch Reynardson, -?-, Percy Ryland, Toby Alder, George Partridge, Eddie Cook. Middle row: Farmer Prout, Ralph Cook, Jack Cole, ? Mutton, -?-. On the ground: -?-, Lionel Alder, Bert Peachey.

EDGE CRICKET CLUB. In this photograph, taken between the wars, are, left to right, back row: Charlie Fluck, Jack Warner, Fred Fluck, Wilf Fluck, Lewis Browning, Rupert Wixon, Ken Wixon. Seated: ? Jack Cole, ? Cuff, ? Manners, the groundsman.

EDGE DRAMATIC SOCIETY. Photographed in the old institute just before the Second World War, the group consists of, left to right, back row: Jane Bird, Mr Herbert, Winnie Fluck, Peggy Birt, Reggie Fluck, Mr Thomas, Mrs Wood, Mr Wood, Miss Minor. Front row: Miss Parfitt, Mrs Booth, Col. Gogarty, Joan Herbert, Mrs Broderick. The boy is Joe Cook.

PAUL CAMP, EARLY 1940s. Situated across the main road from the church, Paul Camp was run basically as a tyre depot for the army. All personnel resident there were involved with tanks. Far left in the back row are Cyril Bedford, Joe Grosvenor and George Moore, who died in 2006. In the centre of the front row is Lt. Parker with, to the right, Jock Ingles, then Richard Painter.

EDGE AND PITCHCOMBE HOME GUARD, c. 1941/2. Many of the men pictured here had already seen action in the Great War, as their ribbons show. Their Commander, Col. Gogarty (centre), had, among his honours, the DSO. In the back row are, left to right, ? Mills, Frank Mansell, Maurice Jones, Percy Guy, -?-, Walter Dainty, Fred Fluck, Bert King, Tom Newman. Middle row: Dan Marsh, George Partridge, Maj. Carruthers-Little, Col. Gogarty, -?-, -?-, -?-. Seated on the ground: Francis Butt, -?-, Charlie Dainty, Lewis Browning.

EDGE WI SILVER JUBILEE, 1944. Standing are, left to right: Mrs Waldron, Mrs Curtis, Mrs Bird. Seated, anticlockwise, are: Mrs Hopcraft, Mrs C. Wright, Mrs Wood, Mrs J. Wright, Mrs Beech, Mrs Cox, Mrs Fluck, Winnie Long, Freda Newman, Gladys Blewitt, Miss Mildred, Mrs Marden, Miss Newman, -?-, -?-.

EDGE POST OFFICE, *c.* 1912. Known as Rudge Post Office, this building served the village of Edge for many decades. By the fence stands Mrs Fluck, with her sons, left to right, Wilf, Fred and Charlie.

HARVESTERS' MIDDAY REST, c. 1895. Although several of the people shown moved while the photograph was being taken, this picture, which belongs to the Edge House collection, is an important one and has been included because of its early and unusual subject matter. Note the reapers' scythes, the stoneware cider jar and the basket of food.

PONY AND TRAP, EDGE HOUSE, c. 1895. Here members of Robert Taylor's family are seen at the entrance to Edge House.

A VILLAGE WEDDING. This fine Edwardian group is by the Stroud photographer Henry J. Comley, and shows the marriage of Charlie Clissold to Minnie Griffiths. It was taken at Grant House, which formerly rejoiced in the curious name of Grunt House.

THE GLOUCESTER TO STROUD MOTOR BUS. This picture is enlarged from a 3 inch by 2 inch 1920s Kodak Brownie snapshot, taken by Muriel Wright. It shows an early Gloucester to Stroud motor bus passing the Gloucester House inn.

FARMING AT EDGE, c. 1945. Here Edward John Cook, of Randall's Farm, Stockend, wears the traditional yoke. He is recorded as using it, during the war, to fill in several bomb craters on his land.

THE MAITLAND COLLECTION. The remaining pictures in this book were taken around 1895 by Florence Henrietta, the wife of Professor F.W. Maitland, Master of Downing College, Cambridge. This gifted lady is believed to have learned her skill with the camera from her relation, the celebrated Victorian photographer Julia Margaret Cameron. After Professor Maitland's death, Florence, who died c. 1920, married as her second husband Sir Francis Darwin, son of the author of On the Origin of Species. Her photographs are important social history documents because they show ordinary people in their workaday clothes, occupied at their everyday tasks, as opposed to the formal studio portraits of the period.

LUNCH AL FRESCO. The first photograph shows Mr Edwards, the local sand-carrier, enjoying an open-air meal outside Stockend Wood.

THE VILLAGE COBBLER. Thomas Carwardine was born in 1818 at Upton St Leonards and died at Edge in 1899. When this photograph was taken he was still working as a cobbler, though it is recorded that he was a man of some education and property and mended shoes more as a hobby than through necessity. He called himself a free-thinker, but apparently had visions of Heaven shortly before he died. He and his wife adopted a five-year-old fatherless girl from Painswick, whose mother was unkind to her. The child, it seems, ran all the way from Painswick to Edge with shoes to mend, whereupon Thomas and his wife pitied her and took her in. She repaid his kindness by looking after him at the end of his life.

EDGE VILLAGERS. The charm of the first of this group of photographs, where a little girl adjusts a flower in her companion's button-hole, is self-evident. The other portrait at the top of the page is of Mary Sims of Whitehall, later of the Pikehouse. The identities of the two remaining characters on this page are not confirmed, but are believed to be Mrs Claridge of The Hole, who was in her late sixties when the picture was taken, and John Gardiner of Doreys.

MR AND MRS EDWARDS. In this second delightful photograph of sand-carrier Edwards, he is seen with his wife and donkey at the summit of Horsepools Hill. It would be difficult to find a finer picture with which to conclude the book.